Giving a Good Invitation

Roy J. Fish

BROADMAN PRESS
NASHVILLE, TENNESSEE

© Copyright 1974 · Broadman Press
Nashville, Tennessee

4221-07
ISBN: 0-8054-2107-6

Dewey Decimal Classification: 253.7
Library of Congress Catalog Card Number: 74-18043
Printed in the United States of America

CONTENTS

PREFACE

In recent years I have had a number of opportunities of speaking to various groups on the subject, "Extending an Evangelistic Invitation." In attempting to prepare for these sessions, I've often been impressed with the scarcity of printed materials related to the subject. To my knowledge, only one book has been written which was devoted entirely to the subject. It presently is out of print. There are a half a dozen or so books in which separate chapters deal with the invitation. Each of them is good but there seems to be a lack of thoroughness in all of them which could represent a real need in the evangelical scene today.

For some time, because of the above, I have felt that something more thorough should be in print concerning the invitation. Conversation with a Broadman Press editor reflected similar interests and out of this mutual concern this book has come.

No one walks with the presumptuous step of a know-it-all when dealing with this vital subject. I think it would be with a keen sense of inadequacy that almost anyone would approach it. It should also be approached with a great sense of indebtedness to the writings of others who have written along this line.

When speaking on this subject in interdenominational meetings, I have found pastors of all denominations extremely interested. Also, I've always found the subject to be of extreme interest in classes I teach at Southwestern Seminary. There is a common admission of real feelings of inadequacy in knowing how to extend an invitation. However, I am convinced that every minister of the gospel can learn how to give a good invitation. Every preacher might not have the ability which would make him a great preacher, but almost without exception each one can give a strong invitation. It is something which can be learned. It is with the hope that this book will add to the learning process that the manuscript is set forth.

INTRODUCTION

The word "invitation" in nontheological language is one which is easily understood. People understand what it means to invite someone over for a visit or to ask someone to accompany them on a picnic or a trip. In theological or evangelical terms the invitation is an appeal to someone to accept the benefits of the Christian gospel. These benefits are numerous; they include forgiveness of sin, a new quality of life, peace, purpose, life everlasting, and many more. Since these benefits come through a Person, an evangelistic invitation is an appeal to accept this Person, Jesus Christ, into one's life as Savior and Lord. As a rule among most evangelicals, the word includes prescribing some specific action in the way of external expression of positive response. The word "invitation," however, is more encompassing than this. It actually includes any kind of appeal to repent and affirmatively respond to Jesus Christ. John Wesley always concluded his message with an appeal for response, but there is no record of his prescribing any particular external form this response should take. He didn't invite people to come forward who wanted to receive Christ. Yet, he extended an invitation. He says in his Journal, "While I was earnestly inviting all sinners to enter into the holiest by the new and living way, many of those that heard began to call upon God with strong cries and tears."

As the invitation is discussed in this book, generally it will include specifying some external form of positive response to the gospel. Assuming that the conditions for receiving salvation have been clearly set forth, the invitation as here discussed, will be an appeal to people to meet these conditions and to openly demonstrate their willingness to do so by taking some specific action which will be prescribed by the preacher. Generally this action will be coming forward to the front of the auditorium as indication that one is receiving Christ.

1 Reasons for Giving an Invitation

I. The Nature of the Gospel

When one studies the message of apostolic preachers, the conclusion becomes obvious that one distinction of New Testament preaching was that preaching and invitation were virtually inseparable. The very nature of the message they preached compelled them to appeal for response. There are no instances of appeal without proclamation in apostolic preaching but there are no instances of proclamation without appeal. Michael Green, in *Evangelism in the Early Church,* observes that the apostles were not shy about asking men to decide for or against the God who had decided for them. They expected results.

The gospel message is of such a nature that an invitation to response is the logical outcome of its declaration. Though preaching is done primarily in the indicative mood, that is, stating the facts about Jesus, the imperative mood calling for response is also there. After his sermon at Pentecost, Peter called on his hearers to repent and be baptized (Acts 2:38). After his second recorded sermon, his imperative was: "Repent ye therefore, and be converted, that your sins may be blotted out" (Acts 3:19).

Jesus frequently coupled the indicative and the imperative. He would conclude a message with "Except ye repent, ye shall all likewise perish" (Luke 13:3), or "Repent ye, and believe the gospel" (Mark 1:15). His exhortation to several followers to "follow me" represents an imperative. When the nature of the gospel is examined, it is obvious that it represents an offer. God makes man a concrete offer of forgiveness of sin on the basis of the saving acts of his Son. Such an offer demands a decision. The good news of Jesus is of such a nature that it demands a verdict.

On top of this, the good news is incomplete without an appeal to respond. The very fact that it represents an offer implies the necessity of appeal. To refuse to urge someone to respond to the gospel would be similar to a salesman who, after eloquently describing his product and his benefits, leaves you without even inviting you to purchase it.

II. The Nature of Man Calls for an Invitation

By his very makeup, man needs the opportunity to respond to the gospel. Someone has well said that "impression without expression can lead to depression." To preach for response and to fail to provide an opportunity for a commitment can frustrate those who hear the gospel and deepen them in their habit of procrastination.

By nature man is spiritually lethargic. He needs encouragement to respond to the offer of the gospel. Paul had a reputation as one who persuaded men and used this strong word to describe one aspect of his ministry. "Knowing therefore the terror of the Lord, we persuade men," he said in 2 Corinthians 5:11. Man's innate tendency to put off can be checked through persuasion. His inherent inclination to wait for a more convenient season will only be aggravated if there is no encouragement to decide. Favorable impressions may soon die if people leave without having acted upon deep impulses which they have felt.

The secular world has certainly recognized the necessity of appeal and persuasion to encourage people to act. All of us are acquainted with skillful and high-pressure methods of advertising. If one watched television for a twelve-hour period, he would be bombarded with scores of appeals to respond. The same can be said of radio, newspapers, magazines, and billboards. There has never been a more invitation-minded generation in history. There is nothing wrong with utilizing this invitation consciousness at every available opportunity for the sake of evangelism.

III. Invitations Are Biblical

From beginning to end, invitations are extended in Scripture. God's probing question to Adam in the garden, "Where art thou?" in Genesis 3 is something of an invitation. The final chapter of the Bible contains an invitation, "And the Spirit and the bride say, Come. And let him that heareth say, Come. And let him that is athirst come. And whosoever will, let him take the water of life freely" (Rev. 22:17). Holy Scripture reverberates with invitations to lost humanity to turn to God for forgiveness and new life.

True enough, we do not find an exact example of the modern evangelistic invitation in the Scriptures, but this fact does not condemn it as unscriptural. Many Christian practices and institutions now in use are not mentioned in the Scriptures, yet we do not consider them unscriptural.

We find no references in the Bible to Sunday schools, young people's societies, women's missionary organizations, church buildings, ushers, hymnbooks, offering envelopes, church bulletins, communion cards, church pews and the like, but who would cast them all aside for this reason? Anything that helps us to carry out the principles and teachings of the Scriptures in a more effective and practical way is Scriptural. The evangelistic invitation does exactly that: it is a practical aid in bringing men to Christ openly and publicly, and that work, according to the New Testament, is the main business of Christians.[1]

Several authors have noted that there are a number of close parallels in Scripture to modern evangelistic invitations. When Moses came down from Mount Sinai and found the people worshiping a golden calf, he stood in the gate of the camp and said, "Who is on the Lord's side? let him come unto me" (Ex. 32:26). This is a clear call to take a public stand for the Lord. When the people of Israel had again lapsed into idolatry near the end of the life of Joshua, he gathered all the tribes together and said to them, "Choose you this day whom ye will serve; whether the gods which your fathers served that were on the other side of the flood, or the gods of the Amorites, in whose land ye dwell: but as for me and my house, we will serve the Lord" (Josh. 24:15). It was a call for public commitment of loyalty to Jehovah. When idolatry was again the issue centuries later, Elijah stood on Mount Carmel and said, "How long halt ye between two opinions? if the Lord be God, follow him: but if Baal, then follow him" (1 Kings 18:21). Ezra, the scribe, called on people to swear publicly that they would carry out the principles of his reforms in Ezra 10:5. Jewish leaders were called on to sign a covenant of loyalty to the Lord after the post-captivity revival recorded in the book of Nehemiah.

Though a number of New Testament invitations have already been referred to, I believe one deserves special attention. It is recorded at the termination point of Peter's sermon on the day of Pentecost. "And with many other words did he testify and exhort, saying, Save yourselves from this untoward [crooked] generation" (Acts 2:40). The word here translated "exhort" is the Greek word *parkaleo*. The Greek lexicographer Thayer suggests that the word means to call to oneself. One can almost see Simon Peter calling to himself those who are willing to obey his injunction to repent. It certainly represents a New Testament basis for a public invitation. It is quite obvious that Peter gave some opportunity for his hearers to identify themselves as willing followers of the Lord Jesus, for three thousand were baptized that day. There is ample biblical basis for the invitation.

It should be pointed out that a number of evangelical preachers have not extended public invitations after their sermons. This seems to have been particularly true of Presbyterian and Reformed pastors and churches which are inclined to be extremely Calvinistic in their theology. To my knowledge the only book in print designed to discourage public invitations is the book *The Invitation System* by Ian Murray. The thesis of the book is that an invitation to come forward clouds the real conditions one must meet to become a Christian. The suggestion is that a public invitation will confuse the minds of those who come forward as to the distinction between "internal" repentance and faith and open acknowledgment that one is deciding to repent and believe. The confusion leads to the danger, according to the author, of substituting one for the other, i.e., of letting "coming forward" be the condition for salvation rather than repentance toward God and faith in Christ. Though the book is thought-provoking, the author has a tendency to build "straw men" and then to do battle with them.

IV. The Testimony of Evangelical History

The invitation certainly has its historic evangelical basis. That is, through much of evangelical church history, there has been an immediate appeal on the part of preachers to their congregations to respond to the gospel. From the fifth century to the sixteenth century there is little evidence for evangelistic invitations being offered. This is due to a number of things. To begin with, vital evangelism was to a great degree dissipated. In a real sense, evangelism ceased to be evangelism. In many instances, because a king or a tribal chief would be converted to the faith, the entire tribe would simultaneously become Christian. The classic example, I suppose, is that of Clovis, the king of the Franks. When he was converted to the faith, he had priests with palm leaves in their hands, dipping them in water and sprinkling the water on his troops as they passed by. In this manner, the Franks became Christianized. Conversion became a matter of mass exercise, and ultimately infant baptism became prevalent in the church and conversion was assumed by the church without a later experience.

The resurrection of the public invitation occurred in the mid-eighteenth century. Sometime after 1760, the Separate Baptists and early Methodists began to employ it. The Baptist historian, William Devon, describes an invitation as extended in Separate Baptist services:

> At the close of the sermon, the minister would come down from the pulpit and while singing a suitable hymn would go around among the brethren shaking hands. The hymn being sung, he would then extend an invitation to such persons as felt themselves poor guilty sinners, and were anxiously inquiring the way of salvation, to come forward and kneel near the stand, or if they preferred, they could kneel at their seats, proffering to unite with them in prayer for their conversion.

This represents the resurrection of the invitation which calls for public declaration of inner response to the gospel.

Invitations to respond to the gospel have taken a number of different forms since that time. In the early nineteenth century, Asahel Nettleton, the congregational evangelist, employed anxious rooms where people who

were anxious about their spiritual condition could come
to certain rooms in the building and receive instruction
as to how to become Christians.

Charles Finney, the most prominent evangelist of the
first half of the nineteenth century, converted anxious
rooms into anxious benches or anxious seats where people
who were spiritually troubled and desired to make a
commitment could come and sit, thus openly admitting
their need, and making themselves available for counsel.

A. B. Earle, the Baptist evangelist at the mid-nine-
teenth century, was the first to employ cards in giving
an evangelistic invitation. He would encourage people
to sign a card in his meetings indicating they were making
a commitment to Christ as their Savior.

Dwight L. Moody came out with the innovation of
the inquiry room. He would encourage people to come
forward; the people in turn would be led to a room
especially prepared for discussion between inquirers and
counselors. It probably represents the most effective
combination of public response and private counsel of
any invitation in the history of mass evangelism.

Billy Graham gives a similar invitation. But because
most of his major crusades are held in stadiums, the
counseling is done on the stadium turf when the service
is dismissed and the advantage of privacy is not afforded.

Local churches have incorporated invitations similar
to those described above. Most Baptist churches have
encouraged people to come forward in open confession
of faith. Coral Ridge Presbyterian Church, an outstanding
Presbyterian church from the standpoint of evangelism

today, asks people to sign cards with a number of options, one of which is an indication of interest in becoming a Christian. Churches of various faiths, which are evangelistically inclined, usually make some kind of appeal for people to register a commitment to Christ or interest in making such a commitment.

V. Some Will Decide for Christ

Because of public invitation, some people will decide for Christ who would not have otherwise decided. I sat one night in Municipal Stadium on the shores of Lake Erie in Cleveland, Ohio. Billy Graham had preached a twenty-minute sermon in a torrential rainstorm. When he extended the invitation, approximately fourteen hundred people came forward and stood in the rain around the infield area.

I asked myself, "How many of these people would have been saved had not Dr. Graham offered the invitation to come forward?" Undoubtedly some would have made commitments where they sat, but I believe the opportunity for public acceptance led many to an initial decision who otherwise would not have made such a decision.

Admittedly, in asking for public commitments, there is the danger of premature response. But this must be balanced against the possibility that failure to give opportunity for decision may keep many from making a decision for which they are ready. After the good news has been preached, many who hear are ready to openly commit themselves. The old adage, "Strike while the iron is hot," is not inappropriate here. Impression without expression can lead to depression and can result in a person's turning away from the gospel once and for all.

VI. Invitations Are Psychologically Sound

There is a psychological soundness in giving opportunity for public response. The eminent Christian psychologist, William James said:

> Once the judgment is decided let a man commit himself, let him lay on himself the necessity of doing more, let him lay on himself the necessity of doing all. Let him take the public pledge if the case allows. Let him envelop his revolution with all the aids possible.[2]

Making a public commitment has a way of putting strength and fiber in a decision made privately in the heart. It is like driving down a spiritual stake that can amount to saying, "I'm burning bridges behind me, I'm cutting cables once and for all; I'm taking my stand for Christ and for right."

In the *Ecumenical Review*, July, 1967, Billy Graham made some interesting statements regarding the public invitation and the attitude of psychologists and psychiatrists toward it.

> I am often questioned why I ask people to "come forward" and make a public commitment! Certainly this act is not necessary for "conversion." However, it has a sound psychological and Biblical basis. I have had many psychologists and psychiatrists study my methods. They have criticized certain aspects of it, but one aspect that most of them commend is the "invitation." Many of them have publicly written that this method is psychologically sound. Certainly, when such churches as the Roman Church or the Anglican

Church invite people to come forward to receive the bread and wine, this too is an act of public commitment.

Dr. Graham adds in a footnote, "There is another psychological aspect, namely the basic human need to confess and pour out one's soul."

There is psychological soundness in coming forward. It is a strengthening factor to men to give them opportunities to openly declare what they're doing in their hearts.

---

[1]Faris D. Whitesell, *Sixty-Five Ways to Give Evangelistic Invitations* (Grand Rapids: Zondervan Publishing House, 1945), p. 12.

[2] Leighton Ford, *The Christian Persuader* (New York: Harper & Row Publishers, 1966), p. 124.

2 How to Give an Invitation

I. Give the Invitation with a Spiritually Prepared Mind

Many of us extend invitations without ever giving serious consideration to the issues which are at stake. There is an awesome aspect to confronting an individual or a congregation with the offer of the Christian gospel. Every soul to whom we present the claims of Christ is an eternity bound person. Their decision about what we offer could and ultimately will affect their eternal destiny. The choice which will mean heaven or hell is made for many during the period of public invitation. These are issues which ought to be prayerfully pondered by the .preacher before he ever goes into the pulpit.

But there is more involved than eternal destinies. The benefits of the good news are experienced not only in the sweet by-and-by but in the ugly here and now as well. Many lives to whom we make the offer of Christ are lonely lives. Christ can assuage that loneliness. Some who hear us have brought the fragments of broken lives to services in the hope of receiving help. Jesus can put the pieces of broken lives together again. Peace, joy, purpose, removal of guilt: all are benefits which can be known by those who make an affirmative response to Christ. The initial step to knowing and experiencing these things can be made during the public invitation. The mind of the one offering the invitation should be saturated with these facts before offering it. This is giving the invitation with a spiritually prepared mind.

Such preparation will be made in prayer. C. E. Autrey says:

> Let him pray until his greatest desire is to see the lost saved. Paul said, "Knowing therefore the terror of the Lord, we persuade men" (2 Cor. 5:11). Lost men are under the wrath of God (John 3:36). They are not aware of their condition. The evangelist knows this and must, by his firm, tender pleas, lead the sinner to realize his guilt before God. Mere perfunctory concern in the evangelist cannot be used of God to bring a sense of dire need in the sinner's heart.[1]

II. Extend the Invitation Confidently and Expectantly

I would address these questions to all who extend public invitations, "Do you really expect response? Are you looking for something to happen?" Every message should be preached and every invitation extended in the confidence that God wants things to happen. Here the simple element of faith comes into play. "According to your faith be it unto you," said Jesus to some who sought his blessing. Many times, what happens when we invite people to Christ depends on what we expect to happen. As Jesus was unable to do mighty works at Nazareth because of their unbelief, so in our invitations is he unable to do mighty works because we do not believe.

On one occasion, a young student of Spurgeon came to the great preacher complaining that he wasn't seeing conversions through his preaching. Spurgeon inquired, "Surely you don't expect conversions every time you preach, do you?" The young man replied, "Well, I suppose not." Spurgeon then said, "That's precisely why you are not having them."

I am aware from experience that there are many small congregations which actually do not hold a great deal of possibility for evangelistic response. However, even in congregations which seem to change little as far as personnel are concerned, there is a frequent opportunity of reaching someone through an evangelistic invitation as well as opportunity for varying the invitation to meet the congregation's needs.

Real expectation and confidence in God will seldom be disappointed. For this reason, in most congregations, it is not honoring the Lord to say Sunday by Sunday, "Isn't there one person here today who will respond to the claims of Christ and come?" Why not ask it like this? "How many of you here today will receive Christ as your Savior?" Rather than "Won't you come," make it "As you come, I will be here to greet you." Let the very words of your invitation express confidence and expectancy.

III. Give the Invitation Dependently

Real transformation of life in an invitation is not dependent on human contrivance, but on the work of the

Holy Spirit. He alone can convict of spiritual need. Only he can reveal Christ savingly. He is the only one who can perform the miracle which we call the new birth. Thus, the invitation should be given in dependence on him. The fact that all of this is his work should be wonderful encouragement to us. He is anxious to do these things. Jesus promised, "He shall testify of me."

I recall in my early ministry that I had great difficulty believing that the Holy Spirit was going to do these things through me. I'm sure that if some analyst psychoanalyzed me he could have found factors in my background which made me question whether or not God would ever use me in the ministry of the gospel. I can recall at times, and I recall it with shame, that I would almost shake my fist toward heaven and say, "O God, we're going to have blessing in this service tonight in spite of you." It was because at that time in my ministry, I had my pronouns all mixed up.

My concept of Christian ministry was this: God is here for me to use in my ministry. Basically, it was selfish. Since that time, God has taught me to get my pronouns correctly rearranged. Now I realize that I am here for him to use in his ministry. And he is very anxious to do this. He yearns to speak to hearts through us. He only wants us to trust him to do it.

Jesus said in John 7, "He that believeth [trusts] in me, . . . out of his belly [inmost being] shall flow rivers of living water. This spake he of the Spirit." For this reason we should believe that the Holy Spirit is going to do his work and give the invitation in dependence on him.

We are channels through whom he works. Yielded to him we give him opportunity to move in the lives of those to whom we preach.

IV. Give the Invitation Clearly

I marvel at times at the clarity with which Billy Graham extends the invitation. He tells people exactly what he wants them to do and precisely how he wants them to express the fact that they're doing it. He is very explicit in giving his invitation and in specifying the manner in which he wants them to express the fact that they are inviting Christ into their lives.

In our Sunday by Sunday invitation, God would have us be clear in telling people what we want them to do in our invitation. When we invite people to receive Christ as their Savior and Lord, we should encourage them to make a specific public commitment of the fact that they are receiving him. Something like this should be said, "This Sunday morning, if you are willing to turn from your sins, and turn to Jesus Christ as Savior, I invite you to slip out from where you're standing and come forward. I will be here to meet you at the front." We would add to this invitation the fact that some would want to join our church on transfer of letter. We should be clear in inviting them to do so. The invitation might be expanded. Others will sense the need of making a new commitment of their lives to Christ.

We should be specific in inviting them to make open and public that commitment. We should spell out precisely what we want people to do. A lack of being specific here can cheapen an evangelistic appeal. I heard of one lady who came forward and when she was asked by the preacher why she came she said, "I don't know exactly, but I'm sure I can meet one of the appeals you mentioned in your invitation." In a sense, this subtracts from the luster of the gospel and can open the door of response so wide that almost anyone would have to come forward to maintain a sense of integrity.

V. Give the Invitation Honestly

All of us have been in invitations where the pastor or evangelist has said, "We're going to have one more stanza," and before we know it one has become three or four or five. Most people in our congregations are still able to count. If you say, "We're going to sing two more stanzas and unless somebody comes we'll conclude the invitation," conclude the invitation if nobody comes. If ever you have the impression that the invitation should be continued after making such a statement, express your feeling to the congregation. Ask them to forgive you as you retract the statement you made previously, but that you have confidence that they will understand. You sense the invitation should be extended just a bit longer. Be honest in giving your invitation.

VI. Give the Invitation Courteously

It is difficult for me to envision the minister of the gospel being anything but courteous. The invitation should be given with the love, patience, and gentleness of Christ. This is no time to scold, criticize, berate, chas-

tise, or bully an audience. In my opinion, you will fail
for certain in your invitation if you attempt any of these.
If there is a time when tact and courtesy are the need
of the hour, it's during the time of the invitation. A true
minister of the gospel should remain sensitive to the
feelings of people to whom he has been preaching.

There is no place for unnecessary embarrassment of
a congregation. I know one preacher who, in an invitation, asked all Christians to turn around and face the
back of the auditorium. That left only those who were
not Christians facing the front. This could be a fairly
rude shock to some unsuspecting non-Christian who has
come to hear the preacher that day. Maybe someone in
that service will be so offended that he will never come
back. Some preachers employ an invitation in which
hands are raised, but make the mistake of putting extreme
pressure on those who simply raised their hands for
prayer. A hand raised for prayer is no excuse for bullying
a person down the aisle.

VII. Give the Invitation Thoroughly

This is just another way of saying take adequate time
for the invitation. John Bisagno, pastor of First Baptist
Church, Houston, has suggested, "I have found that 90
percent of the converts come forward after the third verse
of the invitation." Do not be discouraged if there is not
immediate response as you make an appeal for Christ.
Sometimes it takes more time for the Holy Spirit to do
his work.

I have observed that there is a tendency in the early

days of our ministry to be too lengthy in our invitations. As we grow older, there is a tendency to be too brief. Reliance on the Holy Spirit as to how long the invitation should be conducted is extremely important. Each one of us has had someone come and say after they have responded in the invitation, "I'm glad you sang one more stanza for it was on that one stanza that I came to Christ." We must trust the Holy Spirit for leadership as to how long the invitation should be held. John Bisagno tells of an experience in his church when nine verses were sung without a single person coming forward. Most of us would have pronounced the benediction before nine verses without response. He goes on to say when the invitation was completed, twenty-five minutes later, twenty-seven people had been converted, including nine grown men.

The change in the invitation hymn might be of advantage here. If you believe the invitation should be extended, exhortation between stanzas of the invitation could be profitable. It is important that we be "in time" with the Holy Spirit in giving our invitations.

VIII. Give the Invitation Authoritatively

There is no reason for apology in extending an invitation. We're inviting people to accept a quality of life they could never find anywhere else. The most sensible thing one could ever do would be to respond to our offer to receive Christ. I have known some preachers who seem to bend over backwards to keep people from thinking they might be trying to persuade them to receive Christ as their Savior. In their attitude they treat conversion as if there is something poisonous about it. It is almost as if they say, "We are sorry, dear friends, but we always offer an invitation for you to respond to the Christian gospel." Or, "We regret to inform you that at this time in our service we are going to sing a song and you will have an opportunity to commit your life to Jesus Christ as your Savior and Lord," Such apologetic nonsense is a disgrace to the gospel we proclaim. One can't help but ask what kind of Jesus they are trying to get people to respond to. There is no room for apology in extending an invitation.

The invitation should be given authoritatively. I have marveled at times as I have observed Billy Graham extending an invitation. You get the impression that he is almost ordering people to repent and believe. But why shouldn't he and why shouldn't we? We have the authority of heaven behind us when we call men to repentance. "God commands all men everywhere to repent" and if we are preaching his Word in his name, so must we. A note of authority or lack of it is one of the keys to a successful ministry and one of our worse failures in giving an invitation. Set your invitation on fire and people will come and watch the fire burn. As we invite men to break with the old life, a life which to many is a life of degradation, emptiness, and bondage, we are calling them to a life of freedom, forgiveness, and newness in Christ. With authority and without apology it should be done.

IX. Give the Invitation Urgently

If we have any concept at all as to the size of the issues involved, urgency will characterize our invitation. The New Testament says, "Behold, now is the accepted time; behold, now is the day of salvation" (2 Cor. 6:2). Until a man responds affirmatively to Jesus as Savior and Lord, he is living in rebellion against him. Jesus is a King who is the rightful ruler of every man's life. Until a man positively decides for him as Lord and Savior, he is living in revolt against the King. People should not be encouraged to leave the service without being brought face to face with their responsibility of responding to Christ. We should not invite them to go away and think over whether they are going to receive him or not.

A classic story out of the life of Dwight L. Moody has to do with an experience in which he gave his hearers the opportunity of leaving the service to meditate on the question, "What will you do with Jesus?" At the close of the sermon he said, "I wish you would take this text home with you and turn it over in your minds during the week and at next sabbath we will come to Calvary and the cross, and we will decide what to do with Jesus of Nazareth." Then he turned to Ira Sankey and asked him to sing a closing hymn. Sankey sang:

> Today the Savior calls,
> For refuge now draw nigh
> The storm of justice fails
> And death is nigh.

The next morning much of the city of Chicago lay in ashes, for it was that fateful Sunday night of October 8, 1871, that Mrs. O'Leary's cow kicked a lantern over and the great Chicago fire began. To his dying day, Moody regretted that he had told the congregation to wait. He later testified:

> I have never dared to give an audience a week to think of their salvation since. If they were lost, they might rise up in judgment against me. I've never seen that congregation since. I will never meet those people until I meet them in another world. But I want to tell of one lesson I learned that night which I have never forgotten; and that is, when I preach, to press Christ upon the people then and there, and try to bring them to a decision on the spot. I would rather have that right hand cut off than to give an audience a week now to decide what to do with Jesus.[2]

X. Give the Invitation Smoothly

Many preachers find that making the transition from the sermon to the invitation to be a bit difficult. Because this is a crucial matter, special attention ought to be given to it. A preacher cannot afford to be careless at this point. It is true that the Spirit of God overrules our mistakes at times and there are unusual results in response to an invitation in spite of our unnecessary clumsiness. On the other hand, a slovenly transition can distract and hinder the Spirit's work. Smooth transition is a matter to be worked out between the preacher, song leader, choir, and accompanists.

Some preachers prefer to close their sermon with

prayer. In such cases, the prayer helps in making the transition. Many pastors and evangelists prefer for the organist to begin playing the invitation hymn softly during the prayer. After the prayer, the pastor states the proposition of the invitation.

A system of understood signals between the pastor and the minister of music is a necessity. When the preacher is ready for the choir and congregation to begin singing, he can make an inconspicuous indication to the minister of music who will be ready to begin singing immediately. After working together for a number of months, the music minister will usually know precisely when to begin the hymn.

Other preachers prefer to go into the invitation without concluding their message with prayer. Regardless of the content of the sermon, through adequate planning its termination point can always be related to the importance of decision for Christ. The accompanist will need to begin playing softly at the proper time while the pastor or evangelist is stating what he wants the congregation to do in response to this invitation. Pompous instrumental introductions to invitation hymns distract from the invitation and should be avoided. When the pastor has concluded his statement of propositions, the music minister should immediately begin to sing.

Whether the entire congregation or just the choir should sing the invitation hymn is optional. Regardless of one's choice about this, the music director should never lead the congregation by waving his arm. This can be a distracting factor in the invitation. Another thing to be avoided is the announcement of the number of the invitation hymn. This can lead to fumbling for hymnbooks and take one's mind away from the vital issue at hand.

It would be a wise thing if a pastor took time to teach his congregation how to sing invitation hymns, even to the point where books are not needed. The words to particular invitation hymns could be printed in the order of service if the entire congregation is going to sing the invitation hymn. Smoothness in the invitation is important. Those who have extended invitations over the years know that what is being discussed here is more than a matter of merely splitting ideological hairs.

[1] *Basic Evangelism* (Grand Rapids: Zondervan Publishing House, 1959), p. 132.

[2] From Clarence E. Macartney, *The Greatest Questions of the Bible and of Life* (Nashville: Abingdon-Cokesbury Press, 1948).

3 Planning Your Invitation

It is difficult to stress too much the importance of the invitation. It is not something merely tacked on to the end of the sermon as an afterthought. The sermon should build toward those all-important moments when people will be asked to decide for Christ. In many services it is wise for a preacher to explain at the beginning of his message that he will be giving an invitation at the close and then move on a constantly ascending line to his time of appeal. In most services, all that has gone before, the singing, the praying and the sermon, has really been done to make ready for the invitation. To this point Dr. C. E. Matthews pointedly speaks:

> How many people realize these facts? It might be said that the majority in the congregation and many of our ministers have little or no concept of the seriousness or the inexpressible importance of the invitation. This fact is revealed in the thing witnessed again and again at the conclusion of the preaching service: a good sermon, but no appeal. The audience stands; the people in the congregation begin fixing garments to make ready to leave; women reach in their purses for a mirror and the powder puff. The preacher,

as usual, in a cool and collected manner announces the number of the closing hymn with the stock statement: "We shall sing the first and last stanzas of the hymn. Should there be those present who wish to unite with the church in the manner in which we receive members, you may come forward as we sing." Could there be a greater tragedy than such a closing of a religious service? It is not inferred that there is any intended wrong in such an invitation, but one is almost persuaded that the devil himself could say amen to such an effort.[1]

Such will not be the case if the preacher carefully plans his invitation. I have a friend who, as an evangelist, claims that he gives as much time planning his invitations as he does his sermons. Watching him during an invitation, would lead me to believe he is not exaggerating his point. For many preachers, variety in an invitation is something they've never considered. Yet, there are real possibilities here; but variety requires planning and there are a number of reasons why an invitation should be planned.

First, major emphases of a message should be stressed in an invitation. If one has preached on stewardship, the major stress of the invitation should be commitment of oneself to tithing or some other aspect of stewardship. If the pastor has brought a message on the home, the invitation should include opportunity for commitment of homes to Christ. Such invitations could include specific challenges such as family prayer, or a time of daily devotions employing the Bible or some devotional book.

Second, when one preaches to the same small congregation every Sunday, a planned variety in the invitation can prohibit a kind of unnecessary monotony in the invitation, particularly where there are limited number of evangelistic prospects. It is difficult to imagine an invitation which does not include an evangelistic appeal. In almost every congregation there are people who have never made an initial decision to trust Jesus as Savior and Lord. Since every sermon is not necessarily evangelistic, planning is necessary if every sermon is going to conclude with an evangelistic appeal. Regardless of the nature of the sermon, this is always a possibility. For instance, a sermon on giving of material possessions can be turned in the direction of an evangelistic invitation by quoting a Scripture verse: "For ye know the grace of our Lord Jesus Christ, that, though he was rich, yet for your sakes he became poor, that ye through his poverty might be rich" (2 Cor. 8:9).

Sermons aimed at comfort and support can be easily turned into an evangelistic appeal by making a statement such as this: "The Christ of comfort and consolation wants to come into your life. He loves you and offers himself today to be your Savior and constant friend." Invitations following messages calling for social involvement can be moved toward evangelism by stating that the greatest motivating factor toward social progress is the presence of the indwelling Christ in one's life.

Third, planning is desirable in case there is an unusual response in an invitation. If the invitation is extended for a rather lengthy period, it is a good idea to have the minister of music ready to change the invitation hymn. This should be planned beforehand. I strongly encourage you, if you preach the gospel, to give consideration to planning your invitation.

One of the strongest invitations I ever saw extended was one into which a great deal of planning had gone. The preacher of the evening concluded his message with an illustration about Robert Ingersoll, the noted infidel from the state of Illinois. He related how Ingersoll would speak in cities all across the midwest. He would preach on subjects such as "Why I Am Sure There Is Not a God," "The Mistakes of Moses," "Why Only a Fool Would Believe in Hell." In turn he would proceed to build up straw men and proceed to tear them down.

One night in a midwestern city after Ingersoll had supposedly exploded any possibility that there might be validity in the Christian faith, he offered a challenge to his audience. He spoke something like this: "I am aware that many Christians come to hear me speak. I would like to ask who in this audience tonight after I have spoken would still claim to be a Christian. After hearing what I said tonight, is there anybody here who will testify, 'I still believe'?" Not a soul stirred. Ingersoll put his hands on his hips and laughed uproariously. He offered the challenge the second time. "Isn't there even one Christian here who will stand tonight and say, 'I still believe after hearing the great Ingersoll'?" Nobody responded. Again, Ingersoll laughed. He offered the challenge the third time. This time from one of the back rows of the theater two teenage girls stood and began to move out the row and slowly down the aisle singing, "Stand up, Stand up for Jesus, ye soldiers of the cross, lift high his royal banner, it must not suffer loss." As they walked, others slipped out from their rows and followed them until ultimately almost the entire audience was standing as one great throng in front of the stage singing in Ingersoll's face, "Stand Up, Stand Up for Jesus."

As the evangelist told the story, about halfway through, the instrumentalist began to play the song, "Stand Up, Stand Up for Jesus," a somewhat militant invitation hymn. By the time he had concluded the illustration, he went immediately into his invitation and invited all who were willing to stand up for Jesus by receiving him as their Savior and Lord by uniting with his church or by completely yielding to Christ as Master to come forward. I wasn't surprised when around seventy-five people responded. This represented a superb job of planning an invitation. Don't be afraid of innovation and creativity at this point.

I. Types of Invitation

Though most invitations involve an appeal to come forward, there are other types which can be employed with great profit. A preacher should have two or three types of invitation in mind and trust the Holy Spirit to lead him as to which he should use. There are several possibilities.

A. Invitation to Come Forward to Openly Confess Christ

In many evangelistic churches, the standard invitation is an invitation to come to the front in acknowledgement of acceptance of Christ as Lord and Savior. This kind of invitation usually involves a word of counsel with the pastor and remaining at the front in order to be presented to the congregation. Most Southern Baptist churches traditionally employ an invitation of this type. To all who employ this kind of invitation, a word of caution is in order. A clear distinction should be made between those who are coming merely as inquirers. It is the opinion of this author that a majority of those who come in response to an evangelistic invitation have not yet had a valid conversion experience when they make their journey from their seat to the front of the auditorium.

Some who come have been led to Christ previously and some have really trusted him during the message or invitation. But many come as "seekers" or as "inquirers" and should be counseled as such. Something said in some sermon or invitation has convinced them that what the pastor is offering meets the need in their lives of which they are aware. In response to this awareness, they "walk the aisle." But the truth is that if they have not trusted Jesus as their Savior, the only thing that's really changed about that person is his location in the church.

There's a desperate need for more than a handshake with the preacher and the filling out of a card. Failure to counsel with a person under these conditions is alarmingly presumptuous and represents an inexcusably careless dealing with the souls of men. When there is any doubt as to whether or not a person really trusted Jesus, the invitation to come forward should be combined with opportunity for individual counseling.

This danger was not as prevalent in the nineteenth century as it has been in our present one. There was a clear distinction made then between those who wanted to become Christians and those who already had become Christians and wanted to make an open confession of faith. Those who wanted to become Christians were invited forward for prayer and counsel. Then an invitation was extended for those who were sure they had trusted Jesus to come and make an open confession of their faith before the church. Our danger today is our vagueness in making a distinction between the two.

B. Invitation to Go to an Inquiry Room for Further Counsel

A second type of invitation which has many advantages is an invitation which makes use of counselors and a counseling room. In this kind of invitation, people would be invited to come forward and either stand in the altar area or leave the auditorium with a counselor during the invitation.

As suggested above, the necessity of counseling for people who come forward is extremely urgent. It is my opinion that the pastor cannot do adequate counseling with every person who comes forward in the invitation. This is true if a large number of people come. It is also true if only a small number of people come if each of the small number has particular problems with which one ought to deal. Having been a victim of inadequate counseling, I am perhaps a bit sensitive at this point.

At age nine I came forward wanting to become a Christian. Had somebody counseled with me, shown me my need of salvation and how to accept it, I probably would have been saved at that time. However, the only instruction I got was "sit down and fill out this card." I was also later told to come for the baptismal service at such and such a time. Needless to say, such instructions did not point me to Christ and even at that time I sensed that not everything had happened to me that should have happened.

Over the years, the conviction deepened that I was not a true Christian. I became aware that though I had the outward credentials I had never had a saving experience with Christ. Almost ten years later, aware of my need of something I didn't have, I came forward again in a Baptist church to "be saved." This time I was greeted with "God bless you, we're glad you came," but nobody took the trouble to show me how to trust Jesus.

A few months later, feeling a bit desperate by now, I went forward a third time with a very deep sense of need of being right with God. This time I was told "We will pray for you." For a third time in my life I had come forward in an invitation in a Baptist church for the purpose of "being saved." Each time I left the services as lost as I was when I came in. Lost because nobody would take time to counsel with me and explain to me how to become a Christian. Shortly after this, standing on the front porch of my house, I understood clearly that one is saved by trusting Jesus and I trusted him then and there.

My own experience has convinced me that many other people who come forward might not know what they're doing either.

Because of limited time and opportunity for counsel during the invitation on the pastor's part, every church of any size should have some well-trained counselors to assist the pastor in talking to people who come forward. My personal preference is that this counseling be done outside the auditorium and not be so rushed that it is always necessary to present people to the church in the same service during which they came forward.

C. Invitation to Sign a Card

A third option as to types of invitation would be an invitation for interested people to fill out cards which would be placed in the back of the pews. On the card would be printed a statement of acceptance of Christ, of desire to know more about becoming a Christian, or any other commitment someone in the congregation might be inclined to make. After the message, in a period of meditation, people could be invited to fill in the cards appropriately. After doing this, those who have filled out cards could be asked to take the card with them after the benediction to a clearly designated counseling room.

Some pastors employ cards as a part of the invitation and ask those who have filled them out to leave them in the back of the pew or some other designated place. The pastor would then follow up by making a personal call at their home to speak with them further.

D. Invitation to Raise One's Hand

In years gone by, a popular kind of invitation was one in which people were invited to raise their hand. When employing this kind of invitation with tact and discretion, it can be of much spiritual benefit to some who are desiring spiritual help. While the congregation is bowed in prayer, invite all who sense their need and want to invite Christ into their lives to simply raise their hands as indication that they are making the decision to do so.

E. Invitation to Pray at One's Seat

Many people who have heard an evangelistic sermon or even an evangelistic appeal would like the opportunity to pray. But, many times they don't know exactly how to pray. The pastor should invite all who want to become Christians to follow him as he leads them in a "sinner's prayer." Having explained to them that he is going to lead them in a prayer of acceptance of Christ, he should slowly lead them to pray softly or silently after him a prayer of this nature:

Dear Lord Jesus, I thank you that you love me and that you died to take away my sins. I admit that I am a sinner and I need you as my Savior. Come into my heart right now and forgive my sins, I trust in you to be my Savior and I depend on you to take me to heaven when I die. I will follow you as my Lord as long as I live. Thank you for hearing my prayer. Amen.

Needless to say, combinations of any of the above suggested methods of invitation are always possible. One might invite people to pray at their seats and to then invite those who have prayed to come forward in public confession of Christ. This combination and a number of others would be possible if one employed the above suggestions.

[1] C. E. Matthews, *The Southern Baptist Program of Evangelism* (Nashville: Convention Press, 1956), p. 93.

4 Psychology and the Invitation

Invitations are extended to people. Every sensible appeal should be made to lost humanity to receive salvation from Christ. From every legitimate basis the appeal should be made. The invitation to receive Christ should appeal to every human faculty possible. Thus, the power of psychology ought to be sanely employed in extending an invitation. Psychology is the study of human nature and behavior. It involves knowledge of bases on which people make response. It is concerned partially with the why and how of human response. Use of psychology is never to be abused to the degree that hearers make nothing more than a superficial response which comes short of genuine commitment to Christ. Yet, if a preacher can make it easier for a person to make a sincere decision for Christ, by all means this should be done.

I. Use the Psychology of Example in Invitations

Perhaps a young couple comes forward to openly confess Christ as their Savior. Stop the music long enough to say: "Isn't it a wonderful thing to see a young couple openly commit themselves to Christ as Savior and Lord. Surely there are other young couples here today who ought to do the same thing. How many would follow this couple in publicly giving their lives to Christ?" Perhaps a child comes forward; call attention to it and say something like this: "Here's a little boy, only ten years of age, his heart was touched by the Savior. He has come forward to receive him. If God's way of salvation is so simple that a little child can understand, surely you who are grown and mature would not offer excuses." This is the psychology of example. After calling attention to the fact that certain people have come forward, start the music again.

II. Make Use of the Psychology of Suggestion

If you're acquainted with your congregation and are aware that there are certain people there who need to make commitments to Christ, employ the psychology of suggestion. Perhaps there is a husband and a father who is not a Christian. Stop the invitation hymn and say something like this: "Isn't it a thrilling thing for a head of a household, a husband, a father to openly commit his life to Christ. I wonder how many husbands and fathers have never made that decision and they're here in this service tonight. How many of you right now will take your stand with God's people? Put your trust in Christ and openly confess him. Come, even while we're singing."

The psychology of suggestion can also be helpful in encouraging Christians to win others to Christ. I recall that in a service one evening a Christian mother came down the aisle with a daughter who was unsaved. It was a thrilling sight to see. I called attention to it. I said simply, "I wonder if there are not other mothers who ought to lead their daughters to Christ, even as this mother has done tonight." Unknown to me, there was a mother there who had an unsaved teenage daughter. The next day the mother spoke to the teenage daughter about receiving Christ. That night, when the invitation was given, she had the happy privilege of walking down the aisle with that daughter as she openly confessed Christ at that service. This is the psychology of suggestion.

The power of psychology should never be employed merely to manipulate people to make an open response. In a highly charged atmosphere, playing on the emotions of people can gain public response which does not really involve the will in a surrender to Christ. Such careless trafficking with lives is inexcusable and an abuse of psychology in an invitation.

There are many people who need your Savior. Some of them will be attending your services. God can use a skillfully given invitation to lead them to make life's most important decision. God bless you as you offer that invitation!

5 Exhortation and Invitation

When Peter's sermon at Pentecost pierced the armor of his hearers and struck a responsive chord, the New Testament says, "With many other words did he testify and exhort, saying, Save yourselves from this untoward [crooked] generation." Though this part of his sermon is not recorded, it obviously was longer than just a sentence or two since Peter employed "many other words." Where the earlier part of his message had been a declaration of facts about Jesus coupled with an imperative to repent, this portion of his message is composed of his urgent appeal to respond to what he has said. The King James Version uses the words "witness and exhort" to describe what Peter was doing. It appears that he was giving them good sound reasons why they ought to turn to Jesus. This part of his message was calculated to produce an immediate response on the part of his listeners. It amounted to why they should repent and turn to Jesus "now."

In extending invitations today, exhortation is still a very viable part of our verbal appeal. Exhortation is a plea for action on the basis of sound reason. There are a number of incentives in man to which we may appeal. Any one of them might bring action since the influences which motivate the will are not the same with all people. There are a number of bases for motivation to action, each of which is consistent with the dignity of the gospel we preach. Several are listed and discussed below.

I. The Appeal to Self-preservation

It is interesting to note that Peter's appeal to his first-century congregation was an appeal to self-preservation. He urged them to "save themselves" from the judgment which was coming on that crooked generation.

Some psychologists have contended that man's strongest instinct is the instinct of self-preservation. What could speak more eloquently to this drive than the message of everlasting life? It is the privilege of the preacher of the gospel to show people that the kind of life Christ offers them can be experienced now and will never know end.

Some today question the wisdom of appealing to the emotion of fear, either in sermon or invitation. Though this should not be our primary basis of appeal, it is nonsense not to acquaint people with the dangers of spiritual procrastination or indifference. Jesus frequently employed appeals which warned of consequences of refusal to repent and believe. I seriously doubt that we will improve much on what Jesus did. The same can be said of the apostles and the messages recorded in the New Testament which they preached.

II. Appeal to the Highest Quality of Life

Many incentives to which one might appeal in invitations will have already been touched in the sermon. Pungent repetition of these motivating factors during the invitation can go a long way toward helping people to decide for Christ. One of the finest appeals is the appeal to discover the highest quality of life possible. Jesus came to give us a salvation not only for the sweet by-and-by but for the nasty here and now as well. He offers, to needy people, life abundant. Appeal to those in your congregation whose lives are gripped by enervating anxiety and fear to exchange these for the peace and joy Jesus can give. Tell those whose burdens are heavy to come to One who wants to help us bear our burdens. Quote Matthew 11:28 during the invitation: "Come unto me, all ye that labour and are heavy laden, and I will give you rest."

Paul Tillich has said that the three basic anxieties confronting modern men are guilt, meaninglessness, and death. Call people to find the answer to such anxieties through Jesus. Ultimate fulfillment in life comes through him. Until man comes to Christ, he is living on a lower plane than that for which he was intended. Appeal to your congregation to accept the finest quality of life possible.

III. The Appeal for Recognition and Acceptance

In a day of unprecedented technical advance where machines have replaced laboring men by the thousands, there is a severe loss of identity and recognition. Many college students feel that they are just a number on an IBM card. This is a serious jolt to human personality created in the image of God. The invitation is a good time to remind individuals that "God knows you and he loves you. He has the hairs on your head numbered. He sees the sparrow fall and you are of much more value than any sparrow." What a thrilling privilege to share with people who feel like an unimportant nobody that to God they are an important somebody. He loved them to the degree that he sent his Son to die for them. He recognizes them as people of worth and accepts them in his Son. This is a worthy appeal in any invitation.

IV. The Appeal to the Yearning for Freedom

One of the loud cries on the part of young people in today's world has been a cry for freedom. Free love, free sex, freedom of expression of all kinds have been demands made on college campuses everywhere. The tragedy is the freedom which people are demanding only leads to a deeper bondage. Real freedom is not freedom to sin but freedom from sin and its consequences. Freedom comes only from Jesus. "If the Son therefore shall make you free, ye shall be free indeed." There is freedom from sin's guilt. Penalty and power in him. He offers freedom from anxiety and fear. He looses man from the fetters of selfishness which put him in bondage. We should appeal to man's longing for real freedom.

V. The Appeal to Fulfillment

Many people who hear us preach sense a real lack of fulfillment in life. They have tried many things for satisfaction only to be left empty after exhausting them all. The French philosopher Pascal has suggested that there is a God-shaped vacuum in man and until God fills the vacuum man will always feel this inner emptiness. Those to whom we preach and to whom we appeal during the invitation need to be told that fulfillment will come only as Christ comes into their life. He alone can fill the "God-shaped blank" in every man. Only then will man know satisfaction in life.

VI. The Appeal to Adventure in Life

A basic drive in most lives is the yearning for adventure. Many people have never understood that God designed the Christian life to be adventurous. He didn't plan the Christian life to be a dull, monotonous routine. God planned for life in Christ to be a thrilling adventure. You can faithfully promise your congregation that if they will follow Jesus Christ as Lord, life will be punctuated with excitement and thrill. As one reads the book of Acts, one cannot help but be impressed that for New Testament Christians, there was never a dull moment. A great loss suffered by sizable segments of the professing church is this loss of emphasis on adventure and thrill which Jesus offers. The problem is not that these things are nonexistent possibilities for those who follow Jesus; the problem is that our people have lost the concept of what it is to really follow him. Nevertheless, an appeal in the invitation to know adventure and excitement is still an appeal one can rightfully make.

VII. The Appeal to Influence

There is hardly a person who does not exercise influence over someone else. When a person decides to become a Christian, he influences someone else in this direction. We should appeal to people to make this decision to receive Jesus on this basis. Parents should be encouraged to get right with God for the sake of their family. The appeal to an unsaved father to "take a Christian father home to that son or daughter" can arrest him in his indifference and turn him to a positive response. Studies indicate that where both parents are Christians. usually all children in that family will become Christians. When one parent is a Christian, about half the children are active Christians and half are not.

People should be plainly told that they are responsible to God for the way they influence others. Urge people to set the best example possible for friends, business associates, and neighbors, as well as their own family.

VIII. The Appeal to Supreme Duty

Someone has said "The biggest word in the English language is the word 'duty.' " It is our duty to do what is right before God and our fellowman. The Scripture teaches that it is man's supreme duty to be right with God. "God commands all men everywhere to repent."

This is duty clearly specified. Some conscientious people will have their conscience pricked when they realize that they have neglected life's supreme duty. This can be an appeal which will lead them to God.

IX. The Appeal to Gratitude

Many people do not realize that in turning down Jesus, they are turning down God's greatest gift. Though the words may sound severe, the basest form of ingratitude of which man is capable is to turn down God's offer of salvation. People who would not think of being discourteous, rude, or ungrateful toward other people become this way to God by refusing to accept his gift of love in Christ.

In employing an appeal to gratitude, it is effective to inquire of your congregation: Have you thanked Jesus for dying for your sins on the cross? Periodically such questions can be used to awaken people to gratitude which will result in their giving their lives to Jesus.

X. The Appeal to the Need for a Friend

Jesus said to his followers, "Henceforth, I call you not servants . . . but I have called you friends." The Bible says, "There is a friend that sticketh closer than a brother." Multitudes of people desperately need a strong friend in life for a crisis through which they are presently passing.

A man whose wife had left him and his two daughters heard the statement that Jesus wanted to be a friend in a situation like that. He had been rather careless in his life of sin previously, but the experience through which he was passing sobered him to the realization of need for a friend of great strength. When he heard about Jesus as a friend, he responded to the invitation to receive him and he found a friend who has been a great source of strength ever since. What a splendid basis of appeal to needy people.

V. L. Stanfield suggests a list of contrasts which fairly well sum up the bases of our appeal to people to respond to Jesus as their Savior. The contrasts he lists are as follows: [1]

1. Assurance .... Fear
2. Fellowship .... Loneliness
3. Purpose .... Lack of meaning
4. Peace .... Inner conflict
5. Strength .... Weakness
6. Certainty .... Uncertainty
7. Changeless .... Changing
8. Forgiveness .... Guilt
9. Heaven .... Hell
10. Eternal Life .... Eternal separation
11. Life .... Death
12. At Home .... Away from home
13. Manliness .... Cowardice
14. Fair Play .... Unfair play
15. Normal .... Abnormal
16. Reasonable .... Unreasonable

Though these lists do not exhaust all possible motives and instincts to which we may appeal, the basic ones are there. Creative ingenuity will aid you to list others and will amplify ways of using the ones listed above.

---

[1]V. L. Stanfield, *Effective Evangelistic Preaching* (Grand Rapids: Baker Book House, 1965), p. 35.